YELLOWSTONE
EXPLORERS GUIDE

CARL SCHREIER

with introduction by ANN & MYRON SUTTON

HOMESTEAD PUBLISHING
Moose, Wyoming

Library of Congress Cataloging-in-Publication Data
Schreier, Carl.
  Yellowstone explorers guide / by Carl Schreier ; introduction by
Ann and Myron Sutton. — 2nd ed.
      p.   cm.
  Includes bibliographical references (p.   ).
  ISBN 0-943972-56-6 (hard). — ISBN 0-943972-02-7 (pbk.)
  1. Yellowstone National Park—Guidebooks. I. Title.
F722.S36   1997
917.87'520433—dc21   96-39319
                                                          CIP

ISBN 0-943972-02-7 (paperback)
ISBN 0-943972-56-6 (hardcover)
Printed in Hong Kong through Palace Press.

🦌
HOMESTEAD PUBLISHING
BOX 193, MOOSE, WYOMING 83012

ACKNOWLEDGMENTS
Design by Carl Schreier

PHOTOGRAPHIC CREDITS
Photography and illustrations by the author, Carl Schreier, unless otherwise noted.
Other photography by: Raymond Gehman; pp. 13, 39, 42, 50: Scott McKinley; pp. 8, 20 (canyon), 43, 63.
Front Cover: Sunset over Great Fountain Geyser.
Back cover: Sinter encrusted pool in the Upper Geyser Basin.
Contents page: Unnamed blue, hot spring in the Lower Geyser Basin.

HISTORICAL PHOTOGRAPHIC CREDITS FOR HISTORY CHAPTER, PAGES 50–61.
Old Faithful Inn Interior: Photo by F.J. Haynes, Haynes Foundation Collection, Montana Historical Society, Helena.
Hayden Survey: Photo by W.H. Jackson, Courtesy the Schreier Collection.
Tourist car, 1924: Photo by Sheffield, Courtesy the Schreier Collection.
Firing gun salute: Photo by Jack Ellis Haynes, Courtesy the Schreier Collection.
Old Faithful Inn, 1905: Photo by F.J. Haynes, Courtesy Andy Beck.
Old Faithful Inn dining room: Photo by F.J. Haynes, Courtesy the Schreier Collection.
Mount Washburn fire lookout; Courtesy the Schreier Collection.
Fishing Cone: Courtesy the Schreier Collection.
Theodore Roosevelt: Theodore Roosevelt Collection, Harvard College Library.
Lake Hotel: Courtesy the Schreier Collection.
Thomas Moran: Transparency by Mark Haynes, The Gilcrease Institute of American History and Art, Tulsa, Oklahoma.
Tower Creek spires: Photo by W.H. Jackson, Courtesy the Schreier Collection.

CONTENTS

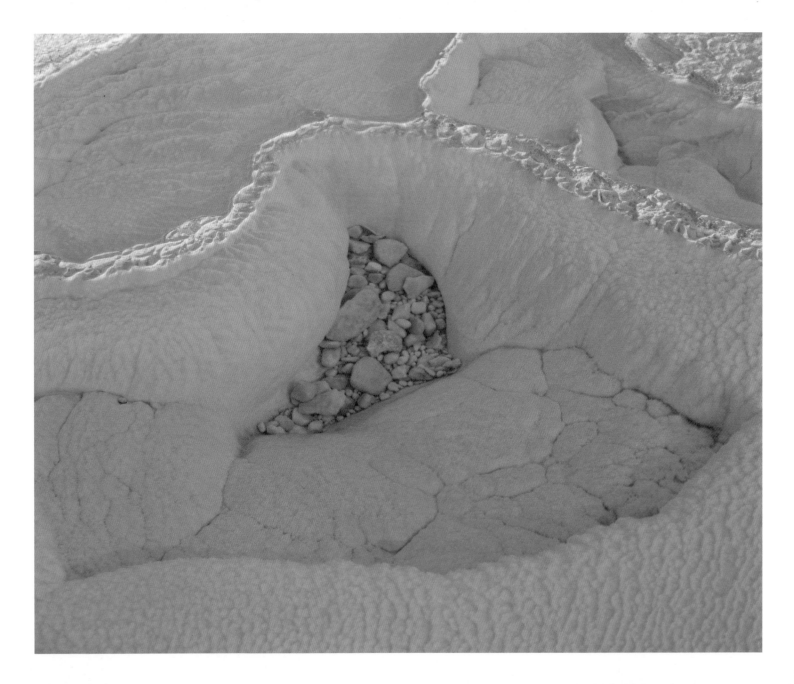

🐃 INTRODUCTION 🐃

*We are now far into the interior and going deeper. We know not what
perils threaten us or what beauty lies ahead. But we are prepared
for anything and we would not turn back if we could.*

Remember those early explorers' diaries? Well, the good news is that such wild places are still open for inspection, still available for what those oldtimers used to call high adventure.

This explorers guide leads us into the interior of one of the world's oldest, best-known and best-loved national parks. To a modern explorer who wants to discover the abundant wildlife, the crystal rivers, gentle forests of lodgepole pine, and steaming geysers in the world's largest geothermal basin, here is an open invitation and a helping hand.

These pages enrich our understanding of Yellowstone phenomena, show us where to go, what to do, and what to expect—facts enormously comforting to travelers unfamiliar with the region.

Still, no one can prepare us completely for the unexpected—and happily so! Unforeseen events are some of the most thrilling recollections of a journey into this mountain backcountry.

And never doubt that there is plenty of the unexpected: song and silence, war and peace, peril and sublimity. Be prepared for anything. There are even mysterious moods that play tricks on conscious thinking: exalted visions that come from the pure air, the high altitude, or the exhilaration of being utterly free.

Here in Yellowstone—for once in our neatly programmed and orderly lives—we can joyously agree with the Greek philosopher Arcesilaus: "Nothing is certain, not even that."

Ann & Myron Sutton
Bozeman, Montana

THE GRAND LOOP

"Grand, glorious, and magnificent was the scene as we looked upon it from Washburn's summit. No pen can write it—no language describe it."
General W.E. Strong
July 31, 1875
(from his diary)

Yellowstone. The word itself invokes visions of steaming geysers, bubbling mud pots, and multicolored canyon walls. Yellowstone is this and more. It is a primeval place where the forces of nature are constantly at play. It is a place where the preservation idea—a philosophy—was born. And it is a symbol of America's reverence for untouched wilderness.

Yellowstone is the United States' largest national park outside of Alaska. Nearly 60 miles in length and width, this immense park is three times larger than the state of Rhode Island. Its elevation varies from 5,000 feet to 11,000 feet. In an average year, the northern end of the park can top 90°F in midsummer,

---

A winter storm over the lower Grand Canyon of the Yellowstone leaves a blanket of snow draped over the precipitous canyon walls. Mist and spray from the falls freezes during winter, creating a large icicle, which encrusts the falls.

while the southern end can drop below minus 45°F in midwinter. Its concentration of wildlife is extraordinary, and wildlife viewing is easily accessible in its vast open meadows.

The Grand Loop—a figure eight in the center of the park—winds among the unique features that make Yellowstone. Follow this road and wander along the Grand Loop among the lodgepoles and geysers. Climb along the divide. Walk upon the pebble shore of Yellowstone Lake. Watch for bison and grizzlies in Hayden Valley, and feel the spray of the Lower Falls.

THE LODGEPOLES

The lodgepole pine should be the true symbol of Yellowstone. This member of the pine family covers nearly two-thirds of the land and is the most common sight along the Grand Loop road.

The lodgepole forest, intermingled with meadows and glades, is the home for most of Yellowstone's wildlife. The forest provides them cover and the meadow provides the food and sunshine they need. Elk are the most common animal that inhabit the forest and utilize the meadow edge. Two large elk herds congregate in Yellowstone to feed among the lodgepoles and meadows during summer. When winter begins, the southern herd migrates south through Grand Teton National Park to the National Elk Refuge in Jackson Hole. The northern herd moves down into lower elevations of the Lamar and Yellowstone River valleys. In early spring, cow elk return to their summer pastures. At this time, they drop their brown spotted calves in the rush and sedge meadows along the edge of the lodgepoles.

Ravens depend on the forest's edge too. Perching in dead limbs of the lodgepoles, they watch and wait for any sign of food. At night, the scene remains the same, only the characters change. Instead of a raven perched on a limb, a great gray owl waits patiently for a mouse or vole to move among the sedges before pouncing on it with silent wings.

Within the upper canopy of the lodgepoles live red squirrels and pine martens. Red squirrels are dependent on the cones of the pine, which they collect and store for winter use. The pine marten is dependent upon the squirrel, and the two live in balance.

Years ago, roadside lodgepoles were associated with black bears, which emerged mysteriously from the dark interior and waited by the side of the road for handouts. They seemed to say, "cookie, cracker, or orange, please." Those bears are gone now. They were discouraged from their roadside begging. Once the bears discovered they would not receive a tasty morsel by appearing along the road, they returned to their natural habit of foraging for their food among the lodgepoles. The bears still are in Yellowstone. They may not be a visible as they once were, but now a bear sighting indicates a wild Yellowstone bear.

The lodgepole region also is famous for its

streams, waterfalls, and small lakes. Trails lead to many of the lakes in this region. Grebe and Wolf lakes are good, short three- to five-mile evening hikes to view summer wildflowers, moose and deer. Grizzlies also frequent this area, so it is advisable to be alert when walking through the lodgepoles. Another popular hike is the Grizzly

Lake Trail, a short hike of two miles. A longer, rewarding hike in the same area is along the Mount Holmes Trail. This is recommended as a two-day, overnight hike, but it also can be done as a very long day hike. The ten-mile trail climbs to the 10,336-foot summit and fire lookout of

Mount Holmes. The panorama from the summit, like Mount Washburn to the east, takes in the entire park. Whenever hiking in these areas during summer, take plenty of insect repellent and keep both hands free to swat at mosquitoes.

Lodgepole pines (right) compose nearly two-thirds of Yellowstone's 3,472 square miles. The upper canopy of the lodgepole forest provides sanctuary for red squirrels and pine martens, while the grass and sedge carpeted forest floor is the home of the black bear (above).

THE GEYSER BASINS

The geyser basins are unique jewels of Yellowstone. No other area in the world has the concentration of thermal features that Yellowstone has. Geysers, fumaroles, mud pots, hot springs and pools are the main attractions in the seven major thermal basins along the Gibbon and Firehole rivers.

The hottest ground in Yellowstone can be found at Norris Geyser Basin. Famous for its pastel-colored Porcelain Basin, this area is colored by mineral oxides in shades of brown, yellow, green, blue and red. It also is very acidic, and the basin is stark and barren, lacking any apparent vegetation. The entire basin boils and bubbles with small springs and geysers. South of Porcelain Basin is a trail that leads through lodgepole pines to Steamboat Geyser, the largest geyser in the world, erupting to 300 feet or higher. But it is not predictable and goes into long periods of dormancy. Echinus Geyser, down the loop trail from Steamboat, is more predictable and erupts about every 70 to 90 minutes to a height of 100 feet. Colorful pools and miniature geysers are found everywhere along the trail back to the Norris Museum.

The Gibbon Geyser Basin contains some unusual formations, including the Artist Paint Pots that bubble and boil in colors of gray and pink. Monument Basin is also unique in that tree-trunk-like cones stand upright in a barren and desolate basin.

The Lower Geyser Basin, including the Fountain Paint Pots and the Firehole Lake Drive, is famous for its pink-colored mud pots. The Fountain Paint Pot Trail passes colorful, bubbling mud pots formed by steam, gases, and mud, while active geysers play nearby. The ground around Fountain Paint Pots is a desolate, nearly concrete-like environment. Most of the ground is a hard pan of geyserite—silica dioxide deposited by thermal runoff and spray. Only a few plants are able to grow on this harsh, exposed ground. Yellow stonecrop and purple gentians are the two wildflowers that are common to the geyser basins and able to tolerate these stark conditions.

Firehole Lake Drive is an unusual thermal basin. Great Fountain Geyser is the famous feature in this area, erupting from a terraced pool about every 12 hours to a height of 75 to 150 feet. The drive also passes White Dome Geyser, an old and large geyser cone, and a thermal lake that is in constant eruption.

Midway Geyser Basin is known for its large, colorful runoff channels and Grand Prismatic Spring. This large pool—the largest in Yellowstone—is a rainbow of color. Beginning with a deep blue center, it radiates outward to pastel blue, then green, yellow and orange along the edge. Excelsior Geyser, now dormant for more than a 100 years, was the largest geyser in the world. When it last erupted in 1888, it reached 300 feet. It still discharges more thermal water, about 4,050 gallons per minute, than any other spring in Yellowstone. Its steam-covered, blue-water crater also is impressive.

The major thermal area is the Upper Geyser Basin, which includes Biscuit and Black Sand basins. Old Faithful Geyser is located here, as is Grotto, Beehive and Grand geysers and Morning Glory and Beauty pools. More than twelve miles of trails and boardwalks pass the major features in the Old Faithful area.

Black Sand Basin has deep colorful pools, such as Emerald and Rainbow pools. Smaller geysers and blue, boiling hot springs can be found at Biscuit Basin. A major feature here is sky blue Sapphire Pool lined with beaded sinter formations.

The best way to enjoy the thermal basins and obtain a better understanding of their function and uniqueness is to take along a guidebook to the basin; several are listed in the bibliography.

In the geyser basin region are a number of hikes leading to remote backcountry thermal basins, lakes, and waterfalls. The three-mile hike to Fairy Falls, a spectacular 200-foot falls, also takes hikers to Imperial Geyser, a large turquoise-colored hot spring. The one-mile hike from Biscuit Basin to Mystic Falls is a short, popular hike to a 100-foot cascade and an observation point. The three-mile trail to Mallard Lake starts at Old Faithful and wanders among the lodgepoles to a small lake where waterfowl usually can be found. Another easy 2.2 mile stroll follows the Firehole River to Lone Star Geyser.

Depression Geyser in the Upper Geyser Basin, home of the largest concentration and nearly one-quarter of all the geysers in the world.

ALONG THE DIVIDE

The Continental Divide, appearing as a dashed line on a Yellowstone map, is the line along the backbone of the Rocky Mountains, along which the watershed separates; part of the water flows to the Atlantic, the other part to the Pacific. This line extends from Alaska to South America, passing briefly along the southern and western edges of the park.

In Yellowstone, the Divide crosses the Madison Plateau, passes near Shoshone Lake, wanders close to Yellowstone Lake, past Riddle and Heart lakes and across the Two Ocean Plateau to the south. For 80 miles, the Divide winds through Yellowstone, wandering among the lodgepoles.

It is impossible to hike *along* the Divide. There is no trail that marks it, nor any sharp ridge that delineates it. It is, however, possible to hike *across* the Divide. The trail from old Faithful to Shoshone Lake climbs to the 8,000-foot Grants Pass and drops 200 feet to the lake. Another trail begins on the Divide near Grant Village and leads to Riddle Lake, through small meadows where moose often are found. For a longer hike south of there is the Heart Lake Trail, which borders the Divide. This popular eight-mile trail leads to Heart Lake and the Heart Lake Geyser Basin. By continuing four more miles and climbing 2,700 feet, the trail ends at the Mount Sheridan Fire Lookout. From there, it is possible to see the entire length of Yellowstone's portion of the Continental Divide. On a clear day, it is possible to see 160 miles away in Idaho and view most of Yellowstone Park.

The Divide is a region of snowcapped peaks, rugged canyons, cold lakes, and clear, fast-moving streams. Winter along the Divide, as in most Rocky Mountain wildernesses, is long and cold. The Divide receives more than its share of snow because it works as a rain shadow. Snowstorms

advancing east are pushed against the mountain range, causing the storms to drop most of their precipitation load before moving on. By the time the storm reaches the east slope, the moisture content is depleted and the eastern slope generally receives about half the precipitation.

Spring is almost an instantaneous event along the Divide. The deep banks of snow begin melting on the southern exposures, releasing dormant wildflowers. Yellow buttercups, pink spring beauties, and lavender water leafs begin showing their colors with the receding snowline. In protected areas—north-facing slopes and ravines—snow and winter can linger until August. In some areas, snow patches will remain throughout the summer.

The small lakes that straddle the Divide part their water in opposite directions. The water that flows east eventually reaches the Atlantic Ocean, while west-flowing water finds its way to the Pacific. Isa Lake, perched on the Continental Divide at Craig Pass, is one of the bodies of water that flows both east and west. In early summer, this small lake is covered with green lily pads and the yellow baseball-size flowers of the pond lily.

Just south of Yellowstone, in the Teton Wilderness, a stream flows along the Divide and actually can be seen dividing. Here, North Two Ocean Creek divides into Atlantic Creek and Pacific Creek. This is one of only two locations along the Continental Divide that this phenomenon occurs, the other being in the Canadian Rockies.

Most of Yellowstone's water flows to the Atlantic side. Yellowstone Lake, nuzzled up against the Divide, and the Yellowstone River are the largest collectors of the park's runoff. On the other side of the Divide, Shoshone and Lewis lakes drain into the Snake River, then the Columbia River, and eventually into the Pacific Ocean.

Isa Lake, covered with yellow pond lilies in July, straddles the Continental Divide and parts its water to the Pacific and Atlantic oceans.

LAKE COUNTRY

Yellowstone Lake extends 136 square miles in the shape of a man's hand, at an elevation of 7,733 feet. Its waters are filled with cutthroat, rainbow, and brown trout. Along its shore are American avocets, sanderlings, California gulls, muskrat, otters, grizzlies, and moose. On its surface float white pelicans, loons, and golden eyes.

Yellowstone Lake is a different world when compared to other regions of the park. The immense body of water even creates its own weather. Large cumulus clouds form over the lake during summer days and, by evening, change into thunderheads, showering the area with sudden rainstorms. Before sunset, the clouds often break up, allowing the setting sun to illuminate the lake and its shore in pink and gold hues.

Another scene is revealed in winter, when the lake freezes over. When this happens, the undulating blue lake is transformed into a large field of white. The cool winds of September hint at this approaching season. In early October, the first snows begin to hit the ground, but it is not until November that snow begins to stay. By late December the lake surface freezes completely, in a matter of a few days. The lake actually sings, like a musical saw, while it freezes over. It remains frozen over and locked up until late May or early June, when the ice begins to crack and break up.

Sudden storms and cold temperatures of the lake make boating hazardous. Small boats and canoes caught out on the open water are easily capsized by large waves, and the ice-cold water can take a life in a matter of minutes.

Yellowstone Lake is situated in a large caldera, of which the lake fills only a small portion. The caldera, or crater, formed 600,000 years ago, when a large body of magma swelled up and created a bulge in the Earth's crust. Volcanic activity began

exuding the underlying molten rock, forming a void in the bulge. The collapse of the crust created the large basin. A more recent, smaller eruption and collapse occurred sometime between 125,000 and 200,000 years ago and formed the oval depression now filled by West Thumb. Glaciers added the finishing touches when they carved and gouged the Yellowstone Lake basin. When the last glacier melted about 12,000 years ago, it filled in the basin, forming Yellowstone Lake.

Yellowstone Lake is the headwater for the Yellowstone River, a major tributary of the Missouri River, and the two join near the border of Montana and North Dakota. The water that originates along the divide finds its way to the lake. At one time, the water flowed south from there into the Snake River, but ridges and mountain building have altered the lake's outlet. The Yellowstone River now flows north through broad, open meadows, over cliffs, and into canyons and prairies on its journey to the ocean.

The lake is considered a fisherman's paradise. Native cutthroat trout are the most popular game fish for people, pelicans, and ospreys. Although a state fishing license is not required here, a park fishing permit is, for a fee. The streams that run into Yellowstone Lake are the spawning areas that provide the lake and river with abundant fish. Cutthroat and Arctic greyling are the two native fish of the lake. The introduction of rainbow, brown, and mackinaws during the 1920s-50s reduced the native fish, almost eliminating the Arctic greyling, now endangered.

Wildlife along the shore also is abundant. In spring, birds migrate here to nest. Molly Islands in the Southeast Arm provide sanctuary for pelicans, cormorants, terns and gulls. To protect these nesting areas, restrictions for motorized and self-propelled boats are observed by boaters in the arms of the lake.

Yellowstone Lake provides a haven for wildlife and plant life, including Hood's phlox (above).

THE MEADOW

Hayden Valley is renowned for its expansive, open meadow and its large herds of roaming wildlife. It is home for bison and grizzlies, while the Yellowstone River, which flows along the valley's eastern edge, provides habitat for water-loving wildlife. Trumpeter swans and white pelicans float along the tranquil water above the cataract, while moose wade in the oxbow marshes formed by the meandering river.

The grizzly bear, a long-known symbol of the American wilderness, is found in Hayden Valley and the Central Plateau region. Perhaps it is not as abundant as in the past, and its scarcity can be blamed on a number of reasons. But one fact is certain: Grizzlies are wild creatures that avoid man's presence. It is a rare event to see one. During summer, grizzlies are in the high country along open, rocky ridges and small meadows where they are difficult to see. In spring, however, just after they wake from their winter slumber, grizzlies stay in Hayden Valley, feeding on winterkilled animals. Here, a chance observation is possible. When hiking along the Hayden Valley Trail (where no overnight camping is allowed) in early spring, it is possible to find signs of bear. The track of a grizzly is marked by the telltale impression of claw marks inches above the imprint of the main pad. Large scat, or droppings, with spring grass and animal hairs also indicate a grizzly has passed by

recently. This evidence alone can cause one's pulse to quicken.

The bison, or buffalo, also is a symbol of Yellowstone's wilderness. At the turn of the century, bison were nearly brought to extinction because of the mass slaughter that occurred on the Great Plains. Millions were killed for their hides or for just their tongues. The only remaining free-roaming herd found in the United States

by the early 1900s was in Yellowstone National Park. Winter is the only season that creates a struggle for bison. Although they are strong and well-adapted to winter conditions, with well-developed neck muscles to clear deep, heavy snow and reach buried forage, stress imposed by cold temperatures, wind and snow does take its toll and cause winter deaths.

Moose are common in the marshy areas along the river, where they can be seen standing up to

their bellies in water and feeding on aquatic vegetation. During summer and winter, bull moose display large racks of antlers. They will lose these, as elk and deer do, in January or February and begin growing a new set during spring and summer—in time for the fall rutting season.

Pelican Valley, northeast of Yellowstone Lake, is another wildlife sanctuary. Like Hayden Valley, Pelican Valley is home for bison and grizzly, but it also is the favorite haunt for the coyote. A walk along Pelican Creek Trail will reveal coyote droppings nearly every foot of the way. The coyote's main prey are rodents, especially meadow voles and pocket gophers, who leave their tubelike piles of earth.

The meadow region is a peaceful place. The serenity and tranquillity of the slow-moving river and the wind rippling across the sedge and rush meadow help create this atmosphere. From a vantage point overlooking Hayden Valley, it is nearly impossible to think of the river as anything but tranquil, but when the river leaves the valley to the north, it enters another world of turmoil as it plunges into the Grand Canyon of the Yellowstone.

The wide-open, spacious meadow of Hayden Valley (right) is home for grizzly bears, bison, and elk. Bison (above) enjoy rolling in dirt wallows that dot the valley. Other water-loving wildlife enjoy the Yellowstone River, which flows through Hayden Valley, providing homes for trumpeter swans, pelicans, otters and moose.

DOWN THE RIVER

After meandering through Hayden Valley, the Yellowstone River begins its remarkable descent through the Grand Canyon of the Yellowstone. During the 35 miles from the Upper Falls until the river leaves the park at Gardiner, it will descend more than 2,000 feet. Along its journey, the Yellowstone River will flow through a dramatic change in scenery, from mountains to plains.

The river has carved a canyon 800 to 1,300 feet deep, 1,500 to 4,000 feet wide and 20 miles long. Rhyolite, which forms the canyon walls, underwent alteration as thermal water worked its way up. This weakened rhyolite became susceptible to erosion. During the past 150,000 years, the river has been at work eroding the soft, altered rock. Harder, unaltered rhyolite forms the brink of the falls.

The river gets its name from yellow-hued river bluffs, not from the Grand Canyon walls, even though it would be appropriate. It was named by early trappers who ventured up the lower Yellowstone near its confluence with the Missouri River.

The Canyon colors change every moment and at every angle. When a cloud or storm passes, the colors intensify. In midday sun, the colors are bleached and pale. The best time of day to explore the canyon and observe its color is in early morning, when the air is crisp and clear and the early light accents the canyon walls. The South Rim Trail provides the best scenery and vantage points to view the canyon. Two trails descend into the canyon: Red Rock Point and Uncle Tom's Trail lead down stairsteps to a closer view of the Lower Falls and the river. Trails also lead to the brink of the Upper and Lower falls, and several vantage points are accessible by car and short walks. Inspiration Point, Grand View, Lookout Point, and Artist Point all offer excellent views of the canyon colors and of the Lower Falls.

Flowing north from Canyon, the river passes Mount Washburn. From Washburn's 10,243-foot summit, it is possible to scan the entire park. The Grand Canyon of the Yellowstone, Yellowstone Lake, the Tetons, Mount Holmes, and even an eruption of old Faithful can be viewed on a clear day. There are two routes up this mountain. One trail begins at the Dunraven Pass picnic area and the other at the Chittenden Road parking area. Both trails are three miles long and climb about 1,400 feet. The Dunraven Pass Trail provides the best views of the park. If only one hike is made in Yellowstone, this should be the one. The trails up Mount Washburn pass through different zones of wildflowers and, during July, it is possible to count more than 50 species of wildflowers in bloom. This hike is one of the few locations where wildflowers bloom throughout the summer, especially late in the season. While the slopes of Mount Washburn display wildflowers, they also provide a haven to wildlife. Bighorn sheep use the summer pastures on the slopes of Mount Washburn, and it is the best location in the park from which to observe them.

The 20-mile stretch of the Grand Canyon of the Yellowstone ends at Tower Falls. Here, the geology changes. Layers of columnar basalt sandwiched between ancient gravel streambeds are visible in the Tower Falls area. Near the brink of Tower Falls, coarse volcanic breccias have eroded into sharp spires. Tower Creek flows between the spires, then plunges 132 feet in a nearly perfect column before joining the Yellowstone River. A trail leads to the base of the falls and, on a sunny day, a rainbow can always be found in the spray.

Northeast of Tower lies Lamar Valley, a wintering ground for bison, elk, and recently to introduced Canada wolves. The broad, open valley begins to change upstream near Pebble Creek, becoming more mountainous and rugged outside of the park in the Beartooth Plateau.

Below Tower Falls, the river enters a much drier region. Sagebrush and Rocky Mountain junipers line the banks instead of lodgepole pine and sedges. When the river passes through Gardiner, Montana, it reaches the park's lowest elevation—5,314 feet. This section of the river is the first to see spring in the park, and the trail along the Yellowstone River is the first to lose its snow and welcome the season's first hikers.

The Yellowstone River, on its journey from Yellowstone Lake, descends into the Grand Canyon of the Yellowstone over two major waterfalls. The Upper Falls, 109 feet high, and the Lower Falls (right), 308 feet high, are two of the estimated 46 waterfalls in Yellowstone.

The Yellowstone River passes along the foot of Mount Washburn, the sentinel of Yellowstone Park. The trail up Mount Washburn (left) wanders through abundant and colorful wildflowers before reaching the 10,243-foot summit. Antelope Valley (lower center), on the northern side of Washburn, is home for grizzly bears, elk, moose and bighorn sheep.

As the river leaves the 20-mile-long Grand Canyon of the Yellowstone (upper center), it is joined by Tower Creek, which plunges 132 feet over Tower Falls (right).

GEYSERS, HOT SPRINGS & FUMAROLES

A gurgling sound, then a splash. Another splash and all is quiet for a moment. Suddenly, the ground reverberates with the sound of gushing water. A hissing signals that the water has reached the surface and is spouting 150 feet into the air. The sound of raindrops indicates the water has reached its apex and fallen back to earth. In the moonlight, it is possible to see only the plume of spray ascending and drifting toward the Firehole River. By the time the mist falls cool upon the boardwalk, water will be rushing down sinter runoff channels to the Firehole.

Only a handful of the nearly 3 million annual summer visitors witness an eruption of Old Faithful at night. To those, Old Faithful

---

A sunset over Great Fountain Geyser creates a vision of its geologic past. Great Fountain Geyser is one of the grand geysers, and it erupts from a large, terraced platform with massive bursts exploding up to 150 feet high.

has a special meaning. They discover a unique display of the pent-up energy below this grand old geyser.

Yellowstone is a country teeming with an estimated 10,000 thermal features. Of these, only 3 percent are geysers. The rest are boiling pools, bubbling mud pots, steaming vents or warm seeps. Most geysers are small, sputtering and splashing and barely reaching ten feet in height. Only six major geysers erupt 100 feet or higher on a predictable daily basis. Old Faithful is one of these, erupting once every 50- and 110-minutes.

Beneath the thermal basins lie the mechanisms that control these features. The most essential element is magma, or underground molten rock. No one knows exactly how close to the surface this body of magma lies. Geologists believe the Earth's crust is less than 40 miles thick here, compared to 90 miles under most other land areas. The zone between hot molten magma and

the crust is a pliable layer of partially molten granitic rock close to its melting point. This zone heats water that has seeped down from the surface. Water filters down through fissures, cracks, and porous rock and eventually can circulate to a depth of two miles. There, it is heated by partially molten granitic rock to a temperature that is above its surface boiling point, but it does not boil because of pressure in the underground network. As superheated water works its way up through the subterranean chambers and conduits, pressure gradually is relieved. The plumbing system traps superheated water before it reaches the surface and cools. Near the surface, when pressure is suddenly released, boiling explosions occur, forming steam. This sudden expansion in volume then triggers a chain reaction that culminates with a geyser eruption.

The natural plumbing system of a thermal feature is located probably within 200 feet of the surface. A geyser must have an almost-vertical underground tube that connects with side chambers or porous rock, where water can accumulate. In some twisted networks, water can cool substantially and ooze from the vent as a hot spring. In fumaroles, water does not reach the surface. Only steam and gases echo up its throat, causing it to hiss and roar.

Geysers are a delicate balance between water and steam, and geyser eruptions vary in length, frequency, and volume. A slight change in this balance can upset the interval between eruptions. A pre-eruptive splash may upset this balance and trigger a major eruption or cause a delay. Man also can have this same effect. Coins, sticks, stones, handkerchiefs, and soap thrown into the thermal features upset their balance and can cause geysers to erupt prematurely, but more likely it causes them to clog, wither, and die.

Earthquakes also play a major role in upsetting the delicate balance of geysers. Near midnight on August 17, 1959, an earthquake, epicentered twelve miles north of West Yellowstone, near Hebgen Lake, shook the surrounding eight states. It measured 7.1 on the Richter scale, formed a 20-foot displacement, and carved out a slab from a mountainside, which dammed the Madison River. In Yellowstone, thermal activity increased. Geysers began to erupt, some with new vigor. Dormant geysers awoke, and hot pools surged with excess water. The earthquake caused some geysers to decrease in activity, and it shut

others off completely. But this is Yellowstone—ever changing, never static.

The thermal features of Yellowstone could not exist without the rock types found beneath the thermal basins. Hard minerals and rocks are needed to withstand intense heat and pressure.

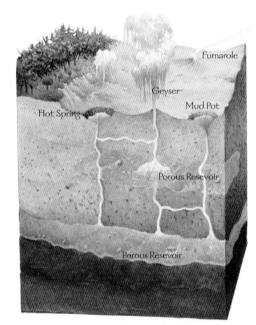

With the exception of Mammoth Hot Springs, most superheated geyser water passes through rhyolite and volcanic ash and tuff. These rocks consist mainly of silica, a hard mineral found in quartz and glass. When superheated water passes through these rocks, it becomes laden with silica, which is brought to the surface. Some of the silica

deposits itself on the thermal features' underground plumbing. The remainder is carried to the surface.

During an eruption, a geyser will splash the mineral-laden water around its vent. With ample time between eruptions, the water will evaporate, depositing silica. Silica forms sinter, or geyserite, the concrete-like rock formation that is built around these features. Sinter can form delicate scalloped edges on hot pools and

Yellowstone's thermal features could not exist without the presence of three essential elements. First, there must be a hot source. This heat source, a magma intrusion, typically at a depth of four to ten miles, heats the surrounding crystalline rock by conduction. The second essential element is water, which falls as precipitation and percolates to a depth of two to three miles, following cracks and fissures. Water collects in a porous reservoir where it becomes heated by the magma intrusion. The superheated water wants to expand. Because of the depth and pressure, the water begins to rise and the heated water moves through the third essential element, rhyolite, a silica-bearing rock, hard and strong enough to withstand heat and pressure. As thermal water reaches the surface, pressure is relieved and water emerges as either a geyser, hot spring, fumarole or mud pot.

Daisy Geyser (right), one of the regular, predictable grand geysers, is where the forces of geology are at play.

elaborate cones on geysers. These mineral cones have formed around the vents of some geysers, such as Old Faithful, Castle, Giant, Beehive, and Lone Star. Others are fountain geysers, which contain a pool of water over their openings before they erupt. Great Fountain and Grand geysers are examples.

Travertine is the deposit responsible for the famous Mammoth Terraces. The mineral—calcium carbonate—is carried to the surface like sinter, but is dissolved in the heated water and precipitates into rinds or terraces as the water cools or evaporates. Calcium carbonate is white or gray when dry, but various colors of cyanobacteria add their brilliance to living, growing terraces, highlighting the delicate draperies.

In Yellowstone, hot springs, pools, and streams are the colors of the rainbow. Bacteria is mainly responsible for the brightly colored runoff channels. Various temperatures of water cause differences in plant communities and color intensities. The runoff channel from a hot spring, for example, is white near its source. Only a few bacteria live in this 199°F water (boiling point at this elevation) and form long hairlike strands visible to the naked eye. As the water cools to 167°F farther downstream, the first blue-green algae begin to colonize. Pigments

within the microorganisms are responsible for their colors. Chlorophyll produces grass green; carotenoids form yellow, orange or red.

Some geyser basins, such as Norris and Mud Volcano, are extremely acidic and noxious to living organisms and other thermal life. These basins are colored by mineral oxides instead of colorful bacteria. Norris Geyser Basin is colored by pastel shades of red-brown iron oxides, gray and black iron pyrites, yellow sulfates, and green nickel oxides. Mineral oxides also tint mud pots the pastel colors of an artist's palette.

Large hot pools radiate with brilliant colors, from deep blue to emerald green. Water reflects its blue color from the sky by absorbing the remainder of the color spectrum. A blue hot pool changes its moods from day to day with the intensity of the sky and the amount of particulate matter in the water. When a pool is lined with yellow sulfur, or sulfur-loving bacteria, the two colors produce hues of green.

Other plant and animal life thrives among the geyser basins. Small black ephydrid flies, probably a remnant of the Great Salt Lake, live on the thick mats of bacteria. They swarm on the shallow runoff channels, feeding on algae and bacteria, laying their bright orange-colored egg clusters on any small stick or rock that projects above the mat. During winter, they live a precarious life in a warm zone close to the water. If they stray away from this protective zone, the cold air could freeze them in seconds. In summer, other perils take their toll. Predatory spiders, dragonflies, and killdeers feed upon the small flies.

The warmth of the thermal basins also stimulates early germination of plant life. In early spring, when runoff is high and the ground is moist, yellow monkey flowers line the hot-spring channels. By early summer, purple fringed gentians cluster near the hot springs. Later in summer, when the basin soils dry, the yellow starlike blossoms of stonecrop appear on the nearly desert pavement.

The scene found among Yellowstone's geyser basins is a reminder of its geologic past.

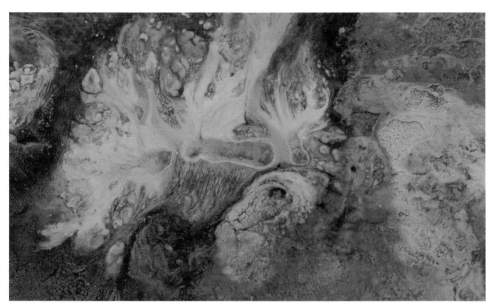

Winter in the thermal basins creates unusual shapes and forms (left).

Microbial mats (above), composed of algae and cyanobacteria, provide a year-round haven for a variety of aquatic insect and animal life. Ephydrid flies (right), vermilion mites, predator, or wolf, spiders (far right), and killdeers all inhabit the microbial mats and live a precarious life dependent on the protective warmth of the thermal water and snow-free winter environment. But the predator spider, like the flies, moves up and down the run-off channel adjusting to extremes in temperature.

Purple fringed gentians (top, right) bloom during midsummer among the thermal basins, adding one more color to the palette.

Today, this is a place of peace and solitude when compared to devastating volcanic eruptions, blankets of volcanic ash and lava, the collapse of a huge caldera, and the movement of continental glaciers.

The oldest rocks exposed in Yellowstone are in the northeast corner of the park, along the canyon of the Lamar River. They date back 2.7 billion years, to the Precambrian Era and are composed of a metamorphic rock called gneiss (pronounced *nice*). This gneiss once was a form of granite, but underground heat and pressure changed the buried rock into a coarse banded rock of quartz, feldspar, and biotite (black mica).

For 2 billion years after the formation of gneiss, the geologic record is blank. Geologists assume the region was uplifted, squeezed and formed into mountains during this period. This sequence repeated itself several times until erosion eventually created a nearly flat, stark landscape about 570 million years ago.

Geysers have built intricate formations around their vents. Castle Geyser (left) has created an elaborate cone built from the evaporation of steam, which leaves a hard mineral called geyserite. Sawmill Geyser (right) erupts from a terraced pool of water.

Shifting seas then inundated the Yellowstone region from the west. The Paleozoic and Mesozoic seas deposited silt, mud, and the skeletons of marine animals, forming sedimentary layers more than 10,000 feet thick in some areas. Mount Everts, near Mammoth, testifies to this vast amount of deposited sediments: Some 1,500 feet of marine deposits now are exposed along the Gardiner River.

The seas that produced the sediments eventually receded. The sedimentary blanket then began folding, warping, and cracking as the Laramide Revolution began 65 million years ago. The Laramide Revolution is responsible for the uplifting and building of the Rocky Mountains. During this time, the Wind River, Beartooths, and Big Horn mountains were formed. At the end of this

period of buckling of the Earth's crust (which lasted 20 million years), intense volcanic activity began.

The geysers and other thermal features of Yellowstone stem from this violent period 50 million to 55 million years ago—when volcanic explosions frequently showered the countryside with dust and ash. Several large volcanoes formed in the Absaroka and Washburn mountains, where lavas, breccias, and light-colored andesite flowed from their cones. Six miles east of Tower Junction, along Specimen Ridge, forest upon forest lies petrified, buried by volcanic debris, later uncovered by erosion. Numerous forests were buried one on top of another. In the petrifying process, a blanket of volcanic material first smothers a growing forest. Then water percolates through the debris, carrying silica and replacing the wood, cell by cell, and creating a buried forest of stone. The surrounding debris has since eroded, exposing upright trunks in this, the largest known fossil forest.

A quiet period followed the violent Absaroka volcanics. Magma shifted underground, squeezing between sedimentary layers uplifting and buckling the Yellowstone region. This peace reigned until nearly 10 million years ago, when more mountain building began. The Gallatin

Old Faithful Geyser is perhaps the most well-known geyser in the world. It was named by the 1870 Washburn party for "its regularity, and its position overlooking the valley." This grand geyser has remained relatively unchanged and predictable since its discovery. Old Faithful erupts about every 45 to 90 minutes, based on the discharge of a previous eruption. It has never erupted, however, every hour on the hour. Its cone (right) is built around the vent with small terraced pools.

Range, in the northwestern section of the park, rose along a series of faults, while to the south, in Jackson Hole, the Tetons also were rising along a fault zone.

The last 2 million years of activity has left the most lasting impressions on Yellowstone. First, several great volcanic eruptions ejected pumice and ash. The oldest eruptions were located along the western boundary of the park in the Island Park area. The road north of Ashton, Idaho, climbs the rim of this prehistoric crater, then drops into the lower floor of the caldera at Island Park. It is still the most visible and impressive caldera in the region.

The most recent eruption and roof collapse—600,000 years ago—formed much of the Yellowstone we see today. A great magma chamber welled up from within the Earth and created a huge bulge in the center of Yellowstone. The magma rose to within several thousand feet of the surface. Around the edge of this bulging un-

Travertine deposits formed by calcium carbonate have built large steplike terraces at Mammoth Hot Springs (left). Cyanobacteria have added their brilliant colors to an otherwise colorless mineral.

Mudpots (right) bubble and seethe as gases—primarily hydrogen sulfide—and steam escape through clay colored by mineral oxides. Each bubble rising up in an explosion is different and unique.

derground chamber, a ring of fractures formed in the crust where volcanic activity played. Lava poured, and hot gases, pumice, and ash were spewed. Dust and ash were blown miles into the sky. No recent eruption compares to the magnitude of that force: It was 7,500 times bigger than the Mount St. Helen's eruption of 1980 and 200 times bigger than the 1883 Krakatoa eruption, which eliminated two-thirds of the 12-square-mile, uninhabited East Indian Island.

The Yellowstone eruption of 600,000 years ago expended a vast volume of gas, lava, and ash, leaving a void beneath the crust, which collapsed and formed a caldera roughly 40-by-30 miles across. Mount Washburn is a remnant of the Absaroka volcanoes and marks the northern rim of the caldera. The tip of the Promontory in Yellowstone Lake borders the caldera's southern flank. Lava continued flowing from the fracture ring for a long period, partially filling the caldera. Cooled lava flows were covered, or crisscrossed, with new flows. Pitchstone Plateau is a lobe of cooled lava. As the toe of the lobe cooled, more lava continued to flow behind it, pushing up ridges. Many of the flows have abrupt boundaries and are more durable than the surrounding rock. In the Bechler region, water has eroded around and over these lava flows, creating spectacular cascades and waterfalls—in fact, nearly 21 of the 46 waterfalls in Yellowstone are located in this region. In other areas, rhyolite—a fine-textured volcanic rock with the same composition as granite—flowed from the caldera fracture rings. This

light-colored rock, in shades of gray or brown, is evident along the road following Lewis Canyon and the Grand Canyon of the Yellowstone. When this molten rock cools rapidly, it forms a natural black or brown glass called obsidian.

After the collapse of the great calderas, when lava flows continued from the fracture rings, the great ice ages began. At least three great glacial periods flowed over Yellowstone. During these periods, glaciers carved broad valleys and canyons, carried and deposited silt, gravel, and large boulders called erratics. The glaciers polished Yellowstone, rounding off the sharp features created by volcanics. Some of the glaciers were 3,000 feet thick and large enough to flow over Mount Washburn.

When the last of the ice sheets receded 12,000 years ago, they left a basin of water—Yellowstone Lake. Chunks of ice became buried in morainal debris, eventually melting and forming kettle lakes or small ponds. Larger lakes were formed by ice dams, creating deposits of fine silt. When these ice dams broke, water gushed down stream beds, eroding them deeper. The streams carried gravel and silt, redepositing it in lower areas.

As a result of this, Yellowstone is a patchwork created by its geologic past. Layer upon layer, it reveals the story we now know. Ancient seas, volcanics, the collapse of the great calderas, and the movement of glaciers are gone from the scene now. Only magma close to the earth's surface remind us of Yellowstone's powerful past.

Steaming geysers replace erupting volcanoes, and oozing hot springs replace flowing lava. That is the scene for now. Wait patiently for the scene to change again; stresses are constantly at work bulging the interior of Yellowstone.

Two types of thermal mineral formations are found in Yellowstone. Most are composed of a hard silica compound called geyserite or sinter, a mineral essential for development of geysers. Grotto Geyser (above) is an example of a hard sinter cone, which accumulates only a mere fraction of a millimeter a year. A softer mineral deposit is found only in the Mammoth area and is composed of calcium carbonate. This mineral can deposit from an inch to a foot a year. But because of its soft nature, there are no geysers at Mammoth Terraces (right).

Yellowstone's thermal features possess the colors of the rainbow. Thermal pools, like Sentinel Cone (upper right), Artemisia Geyser (center left), Turban Geyser (center right) and Morning Glory Pool (lower right) reflect blue from the color spectrum, while colorful cyanobacteria adds orange and green to the runoff channels of Grand Prismatic (upper center) and Cistern Spring (lower left).

Geysers come in all sizes and shapes. Pink Cone Geyser (lower center) is a perfect example of a medium-sized geyser, while a small, unnamed bead geyser in the lower geyser basin (center) sputters only a couple of inches. An unnamed geyser (upper left) at Norris' Porcelain Basin has formed delicate patterns around its vent.

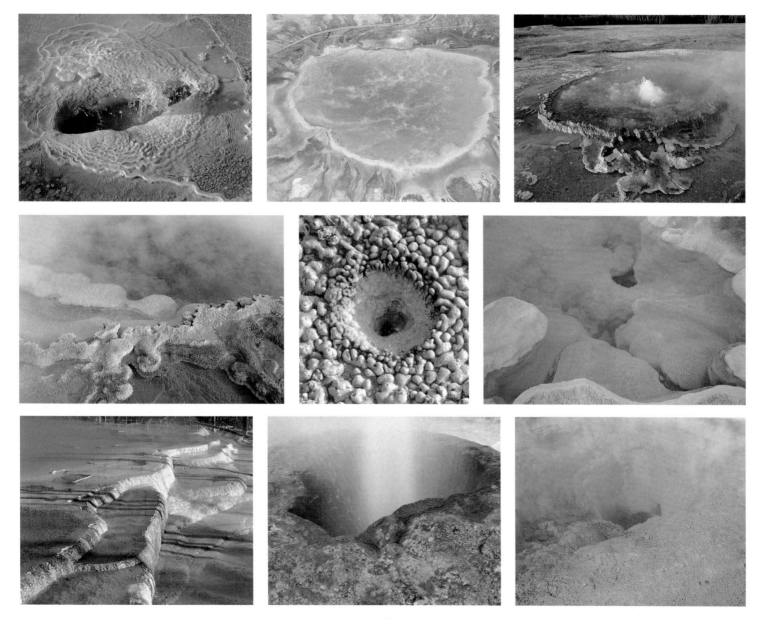

🐃 THROUGH THE WILDERNESS 🐃

"I think a more confirmed set of sceptics never went out into the wilderness than those who composed our party, and never was a party more completely surprised and captivated with the wonders of nature."

Cornelius Hedges
November 9, 1870
(from the Helena Daily Herald)

All morning we kept waiting for the rain to subside long enough for the two of us to escape onto Yellowstone Lake. The rain kept falling onto the Grant Village Visitor's Center porch, forming large puddles on the walkways. The large pounding raindrops danced on the surface of the deck, hypnotizing us into a trance.

I sat inside the visitor's center waiting for the rain and mist to rise, listening to a recorded program titled *The Wilderness Call*. "You are on the threshold of one of the last great remaining wildernesses in America," the narrator said. "Untamed, unspoiled, it spills across the landscape. The tall stands of spruce and pine, the

---

The region south of Yellowstone Lake constitutes one of the largest roadless wilderness areas outside of Alaska. Yellowstone Lake also is an unexplored wilderness region, with 136 square miles of surface area, 110 miles of shoreline and nearly 350 feet deep.

lush meadows and the still lake are there to satisfy the inner craving man has always had for wilderness. . . . Here man does not dominate the wilderness, he becomes a part of it."

Here I am surrounded by wilderness. Not just the wilderness of water or lodgepole pines, but of all natural things: the call of a loon on Yellowstone Lake, a warm shower from a Bechler waterfall, the fishy odor of the Yellowstone River, the vista from Mt. Holmes, or the feeling of open space during a hike up Pelican Valley. These are the qualities of wilderness that surround me.

Just beyond the large picture window, I can see my canoe, covered by a sheet of plastic, resting on the shore of Yellowstone Lake. Everything is set to go. Everything, that is, except the weather. By mid-morning, the gray sky begins to clear and only a remnant of mist clings to the lake. The sun begins to penetrate through the low clouds, causing us to shed our sweaters as it becomes warm and muggy. I carefully fold the

plastic and slip it under the stern seat, along with my sweater, camera gear, and snacks.

A friend is joining me on this 40-mile, five-day canoe trip along the shore of Yellowstone Lake. With him in the bow, I push off from the black, sandy shore straddling the stern until I arrange my awkward legs into a comfortable position. The paddles dip into the water and we are propelled from the shore. The sandy lake bottom slips by and soon is lost in the deep, black water. We navigate along the shore to protect us from sudden winds, and as a precaution should we capsize. It is a great feeling to glide over crystal water beneath blue skies splotched with large cumulous clouds.

Our morning delay now causes us to push the paddle. To reach our campsite on Wolf Point before dark, we must paddle ten miles. But we do not mind. We are fresh and eager.

The lodgepole pines and subalpine firs line the shore to the water's edge, where waves lap against fallen, weathered trunks. Below the water lie brown skeletons of trees strewn like pick-up sticks. We glide effortlessly over these, leaving rippled water in our wake. The sun is unblocked now and glares on our backs. Ahead, to the east, the water is blue, and in the distance, black. To the west, behind us, the water glimmers silver and brown.

We have no watches; only by gauging the progress of the sun can we tell time. The sun is close to the horizon when we reach Breeze Point. As we pass a spit on Breeze Point, we get our first view of Dot Island, illuminated by the setting sun.

The early voyagers would have mocked our style of canoeing. Our long, deep powerful strokes—as compared to the Indian style of quick short strokes—begin to tire us. Even with our style of paddling, we have been able to keep a smooth track as we follow the shoreline. Suddenly, we are fighting the wind and our canoe pitches from side to side. Our track is no longer a smooth path, but deviates to hug the shore and cut the wind to the best advantage.

The sun now has set. With only twilight to guide us, we make our way along the shore. The moon will not rise until midnight. When twilight vanishes, we will have to find our campsite in the dark. We glide into darkness in the shadow of trees. We feel our way in the dark. It is a choice of either calm water along the dark shore or choppy water beyond the shadow. We are alert, open-eyed, as we hug the shore for safety. Our progress has slowed in the dim light. We follow the shoreline and remember the map we so carefully studied before our journey. We know we must follow the shore due south to the end of a spit. But in the dark, all directions seem to be south; only intuition leads us in the right direction.

The silhouette of the spit becomes visible to

our right. On the other side of the spit is our campsite. The canoe obeys our commands and makes the sharp turn. We misjudge a safe distance from the spit's end, and the canoe scrapes against a rock. With our paddles, we push against the bottom and clear the spit. Several hard strokes propel us farther along the shore. We pull in our paddles and glide effortlessly onto the beach. The bow rests on fine sand, where Jim jumps out, pulling the bow to higher ground. This is our campsite. We are both tired and exhausted, but to make ourselves comfortable, camp must be made. First we scrounge for driftwood along the shore by feeling in the dark. The fire grows to illuminate the area enough to allow us to find more wood to build up the fire. With a pot of stew heating on a bed of hot coals, we pitch the tent nearby.

Now that we are still, the mosquitoes have caught up with us. We huddle closer to the fire to avoid them, but even the smoke does not drive all of them away. Dinner is gulped down, mosquitoes sticking to each spoonful of stew. No matter how many we kill, there are always reinforcements.

After dinner, I walk along the shore and look back at the golden glow of the fire and the flickering light against the canoe and tent. I look away to allow my eyes to adjust to the dark. Mosquitoes buzz in my ears, and I am constantly brushing them away from my face. But beyond the

---

Balsamroot (above) dot the hillsides around Yellowstone Lake in early summer.

From Langford Cairn (right) is the view of the Southeast Arm of the lake. It has always been a remote, isolated region. Only by canoeing the southern arms of the lake or by hiking the Thorofare Trail is it accessible.

buzz are the sounds of the night. A great gray owl's deep, resonant *who-hoo-hoo* filters from down the shore. The water laps at my feet while plopping sounds in the lake indicate a fish rising to the surface. The pines have their own sounds too: a creak, a moan, a wisp of wind through the needles.

Fortified with a breakfast of granola and powdered milk, we begin an early day when the lake is calm and serene. We will cross the first of three fingers of the lake to Plover Point. With our early morning departure, we hope to cross the Flat Mountain Arm before mid-morning winds begin to pick up speed. For the first time, we will be in open, unprotected water. If the winds pick up before we cross, we then must wait until evening, when they usually subside. If this happens, we must find our next campsite in the dark again.

In the morning light, we pack up camp and prepare the canoe, while buffalo gnats do their molecular dance around our heads. Small bands of mist cling to the lake between us and Frank Island, backlit by the rising sun. A loon wails, cracking the morning silence. We push off; the bow of the canoe slices the water, and we dip our paddles into the lake.

We had hoped to see wildlife along the shore.

A moose, elk, bear, or even a muskrat would do. Meanwhile, we know there is a loon cruising out there in the mist, and his presence satisfies us. A "plop" alerts us to concentric rings on our port side. When a loon dives, one cannot tell where he will reappear again. He may travel underwater and surface far down the lake, or he may break the surface where he made his dive. We watch patiently, and he surfaces in the path of our canoe. He is wary of us, turns away, and dives again. He streams along, a foot below the surface, neck extended, wings held tight against his body, his large webbed feet driving. A continuous trail of bubbles flows from his bill to the surface. With a slight kick of his webbed feet, he dives deeper. Loons have been known to dive 200 feet and stay under as long as two or three minutes. Again, we watch patiently for him to reappear, perhaps with a fish. But when he does appear, he is far down the lake and his bill is empty.

With little help, the canoe glides smoothly as we maneuver it from the safety of the shore to cross Flat Mountain Arm. The lake is calm, and we feel confident about our crossing. Nevertheless, we tighten our life-jacket straps and paddle harder to cross as fast as we can. The mist is gone now, and light reflects and glares from every direction. Polarizing sunglasses reduce the glare, but most of the light is reflected from the lake, shining under my glasses, causing me to squint.

Directly ahead along the skyline is Mt. Doane, named after a member of the Langford-Washburn Expedition of 1870. The ridges and mountains that make up the horizon to the east and south vary in different shades of blue, while to the north and west, the skyline is

Winter in Yellowstone locks up a cold, hostile, but magical and beautiful wilderness for nearly half of the year. On the shores of Yellowstone Lake (right) winter snow and winds race across the frozen surface of the lake blasting the first trees it encounters. While in more protected valleys, aided by thermal streams, elk (above) seek protection from winter elements.

relatively low and gentle. We are gliding along the southeast edge of a large caldera, and Yellowstone Lake only fills an eighth of it.

Frank Island, to our north, blocks the view of Pelican Valley. This broad, open valley is a haven for coyotes, bison, and grizzly bears. There could be a coyote, right now, loping along a familiar trail with his head low, searching for scents, unaware that above him a peregrine falcon is perched on the dead uppermost branches of a limber pine, head cocked, watching him pass. At the mouth of the valley, a herd of buffalo could be running to escape biting flies—running in single-file, moving down an embankment, crossing Pelican Creek, and lumbering up the opposing side, water splashing and sedges bending to their movement.

We paddle on. Plover Point now is in sight and we follow the shore

The eastern shore of Yellowstone Lake receives the full force of prevailing winds from the west and southwest. These hard, bitter winds twist and distort whitebark pine trees (left) into unusual shapes and forms. Ravens (above), one of the more common resident birds in Yellowstone, take advantage of gnarled treetops, used as observation perches to monitor their domain.

once again for safety. By noon, we have arrived at our campsite, and we are thankful for the smooth, calm water during our crossing. I reestablish my land legs and explore Plover Point. Along the shoreline, I find tracks; some are old and others are fresh. A moose track is superimposed on an old bear track. Moose tracks and pellets are abundant everywhere. Even the willows are indicators that moose have been here. The char-

acteristic hourglass shape of the willows tells that hungry moose have browsed on everything in their reach. A pile of fish scales and bones on top of a stone are the remains of an otter's lunch. Farther down the shore is a dead moose. It probably drowned and washed up on shore. Moose have been sighted swimming ten miles from shore. Some become confused and exhausted and

drown, and this appears to be the case with this moose.

On our third day out, we cross the second finger of Yellowstone Lake, the South Arm. Again, we are up at sunrise, crossing while the lake is calm. We paddle down the arm to its narrowest constriction and cross as fast as we can. A slight breeze is coming up the arm, and we head into it.

It is cool in the morning light, but we know that by midday we will be warm. By now, we paddle at a pace that is not tiring. At night, our arms are tired and feel as though they are still swinging, but back in the canoe, they take up the rhythm of the lake.

The Promontory separates the South and Southeast arms, and we follow it in the midday sun. The glare and heat are tremendous, and the life preserver only makes me more uncomfortable. My mind wanders while my arms stroke. I think about a cool dip but will not take it here. I know the water is too cold, and if we should capsize, hypothermia would set in about fifteen minutes and life would be short after that.

What I think about is a hike I made into the Bechler region. I remember walking through a sedge- and rush- filled meadow, rich with marsh life. Common snipes flew from the trail, startled at my approach, and a garter, or ribbon snake, slithered to the side of the trail to avoid my presence. It was mating season for the dragon and damsel flies, and they clustered on the moist areas of the trail or on the ends of prominent rush stems. The red-bodied males chased the brown-bodied females in the sedges with a fluttering and clashing of transparent wings against the sedge and rush stems. Some would congregate—twenty five or more—on the moist soil. All along the trail, I saw these clusters as I continued to Dunanda Falls.

I felt a relief when I reached the lodgepole-pine forest. The trees provided protection from the sun and breeze—a pleasant change from the hot, humid meadow. But this forest edge also provided sanctuary for mosquitoes and biting flies. I was constantly brushing my arms and legs and looking at my shoulders to rid myself of their persistent attacks. Once I was beyond the forest-meadow edge, the mosquitoes began to thin, and I once again became immersed in my surroundings.

The trail ascended the mouth of the canyon, passing through waist-high bracken ferns. Just over a small rise, I came to Dunanda Falls, which plunged more than 150 feet into the canyon below.

Just down the trail, Silver Scarf Falls, a 200-foot cascade, tumbles from the plateau above. The water is warm, about 85°F, and pleasant for bathing. I stripped and stood in the cascades, allowing the water to flow over my shoulders and

down to my feet, relieving mosquito bites and relaxing tired muscles and aching feet.

Before I realize it, we have reached the end of the Promontory and our campsite. The sun

draines our energy, and all we can do is lie in the shade of a tree and nap.

The Promontory is the Picadilly Circus of Yellowstone Lake. All forms of bird life seem to pass this point. California gulls scream and swarm in swirling white clouds above us. In the distance,

a group of white pelicans skim the water, heading down the arm of the lake. At the end of the Southeast Arm are two small, rocky islands, rising barely six feet above the lake and averaging one acre each. The major bird rookery in Yellowstone is on these two islands. Young California gulls, white pelicans, double-crested cormorants, and caspian terns cover the small islands. Vegetation is scarce. The islands would be lifeless were it not for the birds.

In the morning, it is cool and the sky is gray. Large dark clouds have formed to the northwest. We fear the storm might arrive before we have a chance to cross the last arm. We watch the clouds and the lake. A rain or wind storm does not need to hit us here to have an effect. A storm occurring over the northern region of the lake can cause sloshing here, like a wash tub being tipped. We determine that the clouds are not moving rapidly and the lake appears peaceful. After consultation, we tighten the nylon ropes, securing a green tarpaulin containing our camp gear, and push off from shore. The water ripples only slightly as we cross the Southeast Arm at its narrowest point. As we follow the eastern

The Bechler river and meadows possess nearly 21 of the estimated 46 waterfalls in Yellowstone. Dunanda Falls (above) is just one of the waterfalls for which the Bechler region is famous. The outlet of Pelican Creek (right) is the beginning of another large wilderness region that awaits upstream, ready to be explored.

shore of the lake, we are able to look into the eye of the oncoming clouds. A steady breeze blows across the lake, head-on, causing us to stroke harder and faster.

To the northwest, in the direction of the storm, Mount Holmes is hidden by the encroaching clouds. This is as far as I can see. The mountains block my view, and I am unable to predict the weather. I now wonder what weather I could see if I were in the fire lookout tower perched on that mountain. Would I be able to see Hebgen Lake and the Gallatin Range from there? And would I be able to look beyond and see a band of light between the horizon and clouds—perhaps spy the setting rays of the sun? If so, that would be a good sign that our storm is dissipating.

A drizzle begins to fall on us, and as I look out

After nearly a century of fire suppression, time caught up with human interference during the summer of 1988. Coupled with two years of regional, extremely dry weather conditions and driving winds, the park seemed to burst into flames (left). After an intensive fire-fighting effort, late in the season, it was only the first snows in September that can squelch the flames, leaving in its wake nearly 60 percent of the park affected by fire.

As the Yellowstone fires moved through the park not everything in its path burned, however. Because of topography, microclimates, wind patterns and prevailing moisture the fire misses and skips around creating a mosaic of burned and unburned patches (above). Since then new seedlings have established at the foot of these burned trees, which having sloughed off their blackened bark now stand—and will stand for nearly a century—as white skeletons.

scattered clouds. As I look down the shore, the beach and trees reflect this glow, and they are more vibrant now than during the midday sun. The air, too, is crisp and clean and smells fresh and moist.

We leave Park Point early in the morning and head north along the shore. By nine, we should be able to hear traffic on the east entrance road and by ten, we should reach Lake Butte, our take-out point. We paddle the last six miles in silence. Our experience through the wilderness has been rewarding.

over the lake, different intensities of rain cause the surface to pulsate in shades of gray and blue. Just as suddenly as the rain began, it stops. The clouds break up above us, and a golden band forms along the western horizon. This is our last night out, and it is fitting that we should have a spectacular sunset to end our trip. The sky is a deep peach color, broken along the horizon by

Yellowstone is a wilderness wonderland where weather conditions change quickly and dramatically. A clear, but red sunset (left) can indicate good weather ahead. Cumulous cloud formations (right) develop over Yellowstone Lake and hint of possible thundershowers.

🐃 THE PRESERVATION IDEA 🐃

*"This is probably the most remarkable region of natural attractions in
the world; and, while we already have our Niagara and Yosemite, this new field
of wonders should be at once withdrawn from occupancy, and set apart as a public
National Park for the enjoyment of the American people for all time. "*
Nathaniel Pitt Langford
January 23, 1871
(*From* The New York Daily Tribune)

"Be it enacted by the Senate and House of Representatives of the United States of America in Congress assembled, that the tract of land in the territories of Montana and Wyoming . . . is hereby reserved and withdrawn from settlement, occupancy, or sale under the laws of the United States, and dedicated and set apart as a public park or pleasuring-ground for the benefit and enjoyment of the people." With this statement in mind and a stroke of his pen, President Ulysses S. Grant signed the Yellowstone Park Act on March 1, 1872.

The creation of an American national park was a new idea—a precedent. Even though the 1872 organic act had defects, it did, however, start a dream. The dream multiplied throughout the world, as national parks and reserves in coral

---

The warm interior of Old Faithful Inn, the world's most famous log cabin, has welcomed Yellowstone visitors since 1904 (left), and to-day remains relatively unchanged (inset).

reefs, tropical jungles, mountain ranges, desert plains, cultural monuments, and urban woods were established.

It all started here—the notion that a wilderness seething with mud pots, a large mountain lake and a rugged canyon should be set aside and preserved for future generations. But the creators who formed Yellowstone National Park were very skeptical when they first ventured into this region. They had heard stories—from trappers such as Joseph Meek, John Colter, Osborne Russell and Warren Angus Ferris—of a country where "craters issued blue flames and molten brimstone." They, like the first trappers, left the Yellowstone country in awe.

The earliest account of visitors to Yellowstone dates back nearly 10,000 years to the decline of the ice age. The early visitors—indigenous Indians, living thousands of miles away from their ancestral Asian origins—came up the river valleys to hunt and collect berries, seeds, and

roots rather than settle and begin an agricultural life. Their visits into Yellowstone's wilderness were rare and brief, and the harsh winters and short summers prevented them from establishing a permanent life here.

Evidence of these first visitors has been found near Mammoth. The discovery of arrowheads and tools indicates that these early hunters traveled into this region along the Yellowstone River. They brought with them a knowledge to use the resources Yellowstone provided. They formed projectile points from the black glass obsidian rock they found at Obsidian Cliff. They also used the natural rock formations, such as cliffs or canyons, as buffalo jumps or traps.

The introduction of the horse—in about 1700 by the Spanish conquistadores—changed the lifestyle of the American Indian. With it, they were able to travel greater distances and trade with neighboring tribes. Obsidian projectile points and bitterroots, a member of the purslane plant family with a starchy, edible root, were two important trade items originating from this region. Yellowstone obsidian, the most important trade item from the West, has been discovered as far east as the Ohio River Valley and as far south as Mexico.

While the horse drastically changed the habits of Indians, it also increased their mobility and range. Thus increasing conflicts and tension among neighboring tribes. As a result, warfare broke out among the tribes surrounding Yellowstone. The Crows occupied the country east of the park, and their rivals, the Blackfeet, the country to the north. The Shoshone Indians came from the south, and they all met on neutral ground—Yellowstone. The only early people who inhabited Yellowstone year-round were a small band of sheepeaters, so named because of the importance of bighorn sheep in their diet. They were mountain dwellers related to the Bannock and Shoshone Indians.

Little is known about what the Indians

Early trappers who wandered into Yellowstone during the mid 1800s told unbelievable stories of "hell and brimstone." It was not until the 1871 Hayden Expedition (right) that the first scientific explorers were sent to report on Yellowstone's curiosities. The findings of the Hayden Survey proved to the world that Yellowstone was a unique area and should be protected. As a result of the lobbying efforts of Hayden and others, Congress passed the Yellowstone Park Act in March 1872.

thought of the hot springs and geysers they found here. It is assumed that they followed the game through the mountains, avoiding the thermal basins and the suspected evil spirits that lived there. One encounter between Warren Angus Ferris, a clerk with the American Fur Company, and his two Indian guides in 1834, suggests the Indians were quite superstitious:

The Indians, who were with me, were quite appalled, and could not by any means be induced to approach them (the geysers). They seemed astonished at my presumption, in advancing up to the large one, and when I safely returned, congratulated me on my 'narrow escape.' They believed them to be supernatural, and supposed them to be the production of the Evil Spirit. One of them remarked that hell, of which he had heard from the whites, must be in that vicinity.*

By the late 18th century, the first Europeans began entering Yellowstone country. The French Canadian trappers were enticed here by the rich prospects of finding beaver. Working their way up the Missouri River, they explored the Yellowstone tributary. The earliest trappers left no account of their journeys into this area, and it is wondered whether or not they discovered Yellowstone's

thermal activity during their wanderings. But from the Indians they did learn the name *Mi tse a-da-zi* for the Yellowstone River. And this, in French, became *Roche Jaune* or *Pierra Jaune*, meaning Yellow Rock or Yellow Stone. This was in reference to the yellow bluffs of the lower Yellowstone, near the confluence of the Missouri River.

In 1806, when the Lewis and Clark Expedition passed just north of Yellowstone during the return of its historic journey to the Pacific Ocean, it encountered Indians, who told of the Yellowstone River and the large lake at its source. But the Indians seemed unaware of Yellowstone's thermal activity.

The first known report of Yellowstone's wonders came from a trapper who left the Lewis and Clark Expedition to explore on his own. John Colter, a Rocky Mountain legend, entered the Yellowstone region in 1807 to trap and to encourage trade with the Indians.

The early years of Yellowstone National Park lacked effective administration and protection. Poaching and corruption were rampant and by 1886 the First U.S. Cavalry (above) was called in by the Secretary of Interior to administer the park. During their 32-year occupation, until the National Park Service was established in 1916 and took possession in 1918, a headquarters was built, poaching was controlled, roads were built, patrols were made and assistance was given as they welcomed the influx of visitors who arrived by horseback, wagons, stagecoach and later by camper automobile.

After his return, he claimed to have seen a large petrified fish nearly fifty feet long, numerous hot springs and geysers, and a great lake. Although he was literate, he left no written record of his journeys, but his stories became legends and were too unbelievable even to other mountain men, who referred to his tales as "Colter's Hell."

Colter blazed the trail for trappers and explorers to follow. Among these were Joseph Meek, Jim Bridger, Osborne Russell and Warren Angus Ferris. In the late 1820s, Meek became separated from his party and wandered among Yellowstone's thermal basins. His stories, like Colter's and Bridger's, were exaggerated, but it drew more attention to the region.

The first reliable account of Yellowstone came from Warren Ferris in 1834. He had heard stories of the great geyser basins of the Firehole River at the annual trapper rendezvous and decided to venture into the wilderness to find out if the wild tales the trappers told were true. What he discovered and wrote about led other adventurous frontiersmen into the re-

gion. Despite frequent visitors during the mid 1800s, the secret of Yellowstone's wonders remained.

Newspapers refused to print what they called fictitious articles, and when they did, they were heavily edited to eliminate "exaggerated lies." Finally, an article in Chicago's *Western Monthly* magazine aroused some interest in Yellowstone. The 1870 article, written by Charles Cook and David Folsom, related the experience of the first expedition into the thermal basins and gave a precise account of their discoveries.

During the year following the Cook-Folsom-Peterson Expedition of 1869, several prominent government officials and financial leaders of Montana Territory also were curious and thus outfitted for a trip of their own. The rumor of

Indian trouble along their route caused dropouts and reduced the number of expedition members to nearly half before they left Montana. Under the leadership of Surveyor-General Henry D. Washburn, the expedition roughly followed what now is called the Grand Loop. Along their route, they named many of the prominent features we know today: Tower Falls, Mount Washburn, Pelican Creek, Old Faithful and Castle Geyser are reminders of the Washburn Expedition.

This was the most science-conscious group yet to enter Yellowstone. Amateur recordings measured the height of waterfalls and peaks; rough maps drawn from mountain vistas outlined the shape and size of Yellowstone Lake; and mineral collections gave a firsthand report of the wonders Yellowstone possessed.

Old Faithful Inn, considered the second largest log structure in the world, was built during the winter of 1903-04. A crew of about forty carpenters and stone masons collected logs and fireplace stone from nearby sources and skidded these over the snow with the aid of horse teams. They completed the inn just in time for opening season.

NORTH ELEVATION

these were Thomas Moran, artist, and William Henry Jackson, photographer, whose paintings and photographs recorded a lasting impression of the Yellowstone landscape.

Yellowstone now was becoming well-publicized, and a commercial interest was beginning to grow. Even the railroad provided free transportation for men and supplies of the Hayden Expedition, knowing it could reap the benefits of future tourism. The outside world eagerly awaited the scientific reports on Yellowstone's features and curiosities. Although many of the specimens and reports were lost in the Chicago fire of 1871, it was obvious to the world that these curiosities existed and that Yellowstone was a unique area.

The three expeditions from 1869 to 1871 found Yellowstone to be a very special place. During their journeys, they came to realize the fate Yellowstone could meet in the hands of a few, but also realized that only the government could afford to develop the necessary infrastructure. When Hayden returned to Washington in the fall of 1871, after the Yellowstone expedition of that summer, he launched a campaign to promote a park bill. With the help of Langford, of the Washburn Expedition, and William H. Clagett, newly elected congressional delegate from Montana Territory, they drew up the Park Bill, based upon the Yosemite Act of 1864, which reserved the Yosemite Valley from settlement and placed it in the protection of the state of

Yellowstone has always evoked curiosity with its unusual features, especially fishing cone (upper left), where a fisherman could catch a trout, drop it into a hot spring and parboil it on the same line. The mystic of Yellowstone has always attracted noblemen and dignitaries. But none have been as popular as Theodore Roosevelt (top) whose visit in 1903 brought world attention to Yellowstone. After that year, the increasing number of visitors led to the building of the grand hotels, and by the 1920s the Civil Conservation Corps (CCC) improved trails and roads, and built lookout towers, like that on Mount Washburn (left).

Several members of the Expedition, including Cornelius Hedges and Nathaniel Langford, began publicizing the results of their trip and, from them, serious interest grew. The publicity of the Washburn Expedition resulted in an appropriation by Congress for an official exploration into the Yellowstone region. The 1871 Hayden Expedition, in association with the U.S. Army Corps of Engineers, was under the leadership of Ferdinand V. Hayden, geologist and head of the U.S. Geological Survey of the Territories. He lead a party of twenty highly qualified scientists, topographers, botonists, physicians, photographers, and artists. Prominent among

California. Yellowstone was a special problem. Most of Yellowstone was in Wyoming Territory—Wyoming was not a state until 1889—and only a small portion was in Montana Territory. It would need federal designation and protection and, most important, federal money to develop access. With help by members of the Washburn party, they began promoting the Park Bill. Hayden made sure the public and members of Congress were well informed about the bill through newspaper articles, public lectures, and personal visits to the delegates. Mineral specimens, Moran's paintings and Jackson's photographs were placed strategically in the rotunda of the United States Capital for members of Congress to see as they passed by them to and from work each day.

The publicity and timing were perfect. While the bill was in committee for two months, there was no opposition. During floor debate, one congressman said, "This bill treads upon no rights of the settler, infringes upon no permanent prospect of settlement of that (Wyoming) Territory." The area seemed so remote and the legislation so insignificant that the bill passed through Congress with a two-to-one vote. With President Grant's signature, it became law and thus created the United States' first national park.

Even though the Yellowstone Park Act was a great achievement, there were defects in its structure. It assumed that revenue would be generated by tourism, but forgot that Yellowstone was remote and only received a handful of visitors a year. Without revenue, the park lacked administration. The law also placed the park under the exclusive control of the Secretary of the Interior without giving guidelines as to how it should be run. The act stated that the Secretary of the Interior "shall provide against the wanton destruction of the fish and game found within" the park, but it did not state which laws would apply or which courts would try criminal cases.

The new national park was trouble-bound before news of the act reached Montana and Yellowstone. Montanans were expecting the government to establish roads and make the park more accessible. Visitors began arriving, though there were no funds for Yellowstone's protection, administration, or road building. The increased number of visitors began putting pressure on the park's resources. Visitors began chipping away and collecting the geyserite formations and started taking a toll on Yellowstone's wildlife.

For the first five years, Superintendent Langford, a member of the Washburn Expedition and a park advocate, watched over the new park. Because he received no salary, he had to make his living elsewhere and entered the park only twice during his five years in office. During those years, the need for a paid full-time superintendent became apparent to Congress. Even with a full-time superintendent, the destruction continued. The early superintendents had little power and were weak at administrating the park. Poaching was

Lake Hotel, one of two remaining grand hotels, originally was built in 1889 by the Northern Pacific Railroad as a simple rectangular clapboard building. By the 1900s, Robert Reamer, the architect of Old Faithful Inn, was asked to remodel the plain building. He transformed it into a neoclassical hotel sporting ionic columns and roof dormers.

rampant and was known to occur within the superintendent's backyard. Other problems arose as some of the superintendents coerced with private concessions when granting leases. Buildings began to sprout near, or sometimes on, the very features that the park was established to protect. Congress finally declined to appropriate money for park protection when there was no protection going on. They decided to take another step. The Secretary of the Interior called upon the Secretary of War for assistance. On August 20, 1886, the First U.S. Cavalry relieved the civilian superintendent of his duties.

Yellowstone now had the protection it needed. The Army headquartered at Mammoth Hot Springs, first in Camp Sheridan and after the 1890s, at Fort Yellowstone (where the stone buildings still house park headquarters today). The Army immediately began improving and constructing new roads—it designed and engineered the Grand Loop Road into a figure eight—and began curtailing wildlife exploitation by establishing and manning a series of soldier stations.

The 1894 arrest of a well-known poacher by the name of Ed Howell was a turning point in the protection of wildlife and park features. Howell was caught slaughtering bison in Pelican Valley, and he was taken to Mammoth for prosecution. Howell was released because of a lack of strong park protection laws. But a prominent journalist drew national attention to the problem of poaching, prompting Congress to create the National Park

The paintings of Thomas Moran (left)—watercolor of Tower Falls—and the photographs of William Henry Jackson (right)—a view of the spires above the brink of Tower Falls— made during the Hayden Survey of 1871 were instrumental in helping show Congress the scenic wonders and consequently the passing of the National Park Act, creating Yellowstone National Park.

Protective Act (Lacey Act). When Howell returned the following year, he was caught poaching, and ironically was the first person arrested and punished under the new law.

The Army held a tight reign over the park during its administration, but in 1916, it was realized that the Army no longer could fulfill all aspects of running a national park. Visitors were demanding information about the natural features. They wanted to learn about the natural science and history of the region, and the Army did not have the skill at public relations. There now were other national parks and monuments established, and each was being run independently. It finally was decided that a separate agency should control the national parks and monuments, and hence the National Park Service was created. The Army relinquished

control of Yellowstone in 1918 to the newly formed National Park Service.

Tourists brought a new era to Yellowstone. The days of early Americans, trappers, explorers, scientists and surveyors are gone. A new explorer is here now—one who delights in discovering the canyon rim, the pebble shore of Yellowstone Lake, a mountain path lined with wildflowers, or the sinter encrusted pools of the geyser basins. Like the early trappers, today's visitors are still in awe when discovering Yellowstone's curiosities. The natural beauty remains—as it was when John Colter wandered among the lodgepoles—all because of the preservation idea.

🐃 BIBLIOGRAPHY 🐃

NATURE

Bartlett, Richard. 1974. *Nature's Yellowstone*. Albuquerque: University of New Mexico Press.

Hirschmann, Fred. 1982. *Yellowstone*. Portland: Graphic Arts Center Publishing Company.

Perry, William, and editors of Homestead Publishing. 1995. *Rocky Mountain Wildlife of Yellowstone and Grand Teton National Parks*. Moose, Wyoming: Homestead Publishing.

Raynes, Bert. 1995. *Birds of Jackson Hole*. Moose, Wyoming: Homestead Publishing.

Raynes, Bert. 1995. *Wildlife of Yellowstone and Jackson Hole*. Moose, Wyoming: Homestead Publishing.

Schreier, Carl. 1996. *A Field Guide to Wildflowers of the Rocky Mountains*. Moose, Wyoming: Homestead Publishing.

Schreier, Carl. 1996. *Grand Teton Explorers Guide*. Moose, Wyoming: Homestead Publishing.

Sutton, Ann and Myron. 1972. *Yellowstone: A Century of the Wilderness Idea*. New York: Macmillan.

GEOLOGY

Bryan, T. Scott. 1979. *The Geysers of Yellowstone*. Boulder, Colorado: Colorado Associated University Press.

Keefer, William R. 1976. *The Geologic Story of Yellowstone National Park*. U.S. Geological Survey.

Schreier, Carl. 1992. (2nd ed) *A Field Guide to Yellowstone's Geysers, Hot Springs and Fumaroles*. Moose, Wyoming: Homestead Publishing.

WILDERNESS

Nash, Roderick. 1973. *Wilderness and the American Mind*. London: Yale University Press.

Editors of Homestead Publishing. 1997. *Yellowstone Hiking Map*. Moose, Wyoming: Homestead Publishing.

Schreier, Carl. 1997. *Hiking Yellowstone Trails*. Moose, Wyoming: Homestead Publishing.

HISTORY

Bonney, Lorraine. 1998. *Bonney's Guide to Yellowstone National Park*. Moose, Wyoming: Homestead Publishing.

Chittenden, Hiram M. 1964. *The Yellowstone National Park*. Norman: University of Oklahoma Press.

Clary, David A. 1993. *The Place Where Hell Bubbled Up*. Moose, Wyoming: Homestead Publishing.

Haines, Aubrey L. 1977. *The Yellowstone Story: A History of Our First National Park*. (Vols. 1 & 2). Boulder: Colorado Associated University Press.

Langford, Nathaniel P. 1905 (1974). *The Discovery of Yellowstone Park*. Lincoln: University of Nebraska Press.

Sanborn, Margaret. 1993. *The Grand Tetons: The Story of Taming the Western Wilderness*. Moose, Wyoming: Homestead Publishing.

Schreier, Carl. 1989. *Yellowstone Selected Photographs: 1870-1960*. Moose, Wyoming: Homestead Publishing.

🐃 SERVICES 🐃

MAMMOTH* - campground, visitor center, ranger station, medical clinic, accommodations (hotel & cabins), service station, restaurant, snack bars, groceries, bar and lounge, gift shops, horse rides, showers, post office, firewood.

INDIAN CREEK - campground.

TOWER/ROOSEVELT - campground, ranger station, cabins, service station, restaurant, snack bar, groceries, gift shops, horse rides, showers, firewood.

SLOUGH CREEK - campground.

PEBBLE CREEK - campground.

CANYON* - campground (hard-sided vehicles only), visitor center, ranger station, motor lodge (cabins), service station, restaurants, snack bars, groceries, bar and lounge, gift shops, horse rides, showers, laundry, post office, firewood.

NORRIS - campground, firewood.

MADISON* - campground, firewood.

OLD FAITHFUL* - visitor center, ranger station, limited medical assistance, accommodations (hotel & cabins), service stations, restaurants, snack bars, groceries, bar and lounge, gift & photo shops, showers, post office.

FISHING BRIDGE - campgrounds (Park Service; hard-sided vehicles only and private RV park), visitor center, service station, snack bar, groceries, gift shop, showers, laundry, firewood.

LAKE - ranger station, hospital, accommodations (hotel & cabins), service station, restaurants, snack bars, groceries, bar and lounge, gift shops, post office.

BRIDGE BAY - campground, marina, tackle shop, boat cruise and rentals, firewood.

WEST THUMB* - hut.

GRANT VILLAGE - campground, visitor center,

ranger station, motel, service station, restaurants, groceries, gift shops, boat ramp (no facilities), showers, laundry, post office, firewood.

LEWIS LAKE - campground, boat launch, firewood.

*Denotes limited winter facilities.

OUTSIDE YELLOWSTONE NATIONAL PARK - All services available at the five park entrances, including West Yellowstone, Gardiner and Cooke City, Montana, and Cody and Jackson, Wyoming. Hospitals are available at Livingston (north of Gardiner), Cody and Jackson, with limited medical assistance at West Yellowstone.

BOOKS IN THIS SERIES:
Yellowstone
Grand Teton
Glacier-Waterton
Banff-Jasper

MORE READING:
For a complete listing of other natural history publications from Homestead Publishing, please send for a catalog by writing:
HOMESTEAD PUBLISHING
Mail Order Department
Box 193
Moose, Wyoming 83012

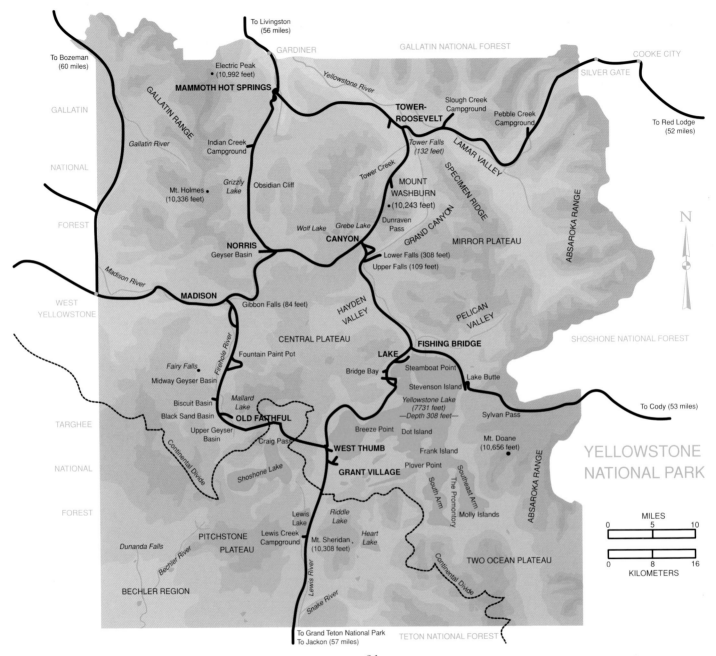

To Livingston
(56 miles)

GARDINER

GALLATIN NATIONAL FOREST

COOKE CITY

SILVER GATE

To Bozeman
(60 miles)

GALLATIN

Electric Peak
• (10,992 feet)

MAMMOTH HOT SPRINGS

Yellowstone River

TOWER-
ROOSEVELT

Slough Creek
Campground

Pebble Creek
Campground

To Red Lodge
(52 miles)

GALLATIN RANGE

Gallatin River

NATIONAL

Indian Creek
Campground

Tower Falls
(132 feet)

LAMAR VALLEY

FOREST

Mt. Holmes •
(10,336 feet)

Grizzly
Lake

Obsidian Cliff

Tower Creek

MOUNT
WASHBURN
• (10,243 feet)

SPECIMEN RIDGE

ABSAROKA RANGE

Wolf Lake

Grebe Lake

Dunraven
Pass

GRAND CANYON

MIRROR PLATEAU

NORRIS
Geyser Basin

CANYON

Madison River

Lower Falls (308 feet)
Upper Falls (109 feet)

WEST
YELLOWSTONE

MADISON

Gibbon Falls (84 feet)

HAYDEN
VALLEY

PELICAN
VALLEY

SHOSHONE NATIONAL FOREST

N

CENTRAL PLATEAU

FISHING BRIDGE

Firehole River

Fountain Paint Pot

LAKE

Fairy Falls •

Midway Geyser Basin

Bridge Bay

Steamboat Point

Lake Butte

Stevenson Island

Biscuit Basin

Mallard
Lake

Black Sand Basin

OLD FAITHFUL

Upper Geyser
Basin

Craig Pass

Continental Divide

TARGHEE

NATIONAL

FOREST

Yellowstone Lake
(7731 feet)
—Depth 308 feet—

Sylvan Pass

To Cody (53 miles)

WEST THUMB

Breeze Point

Dot Island

Mt. Doane
(10,656 feet) •

GRANT VILLAGE

Frank Island

Plover Point

ABSAROKA RANGE

YELLOWSTONE
NATIONAL
PARK

Shoshone Lake

South Arm

The Promontory

Southeast Arm

Molly Islands

MILES

0   5   10

Lewis
Lake

Riddle
Lake

Heart
Lake

0   8   16

KILOMETERS

Dunanda Falls

Lewis Creek
Campground

Mt. Sheridan
(10,308 feet)

PITCHSTONE
PLATEAU

Bechler River

Lewis River

Continental Divide

TWO OCEAN PLATEAU

BECHLER REGION

Snake River

To Grand Teton National Park
To Jackon (57 miles)

TETON NATIONAL FOREST